PowerPoint for Beginners

POWERPOINT ESSENTIALS BOOK 1

M.L. HUMPHREY

ISBN: 1721986146
ISBN-13: 978-1721986149

SELECT TITLES BY M.L. HUMPHREY

WORD ESSENTIALS
Word for Beginners
Intermediate Word

POWERPOINT ESSENTIALS
PowerPoint for Beginners
Intermediate PowerPoint

EXCEL ESSENTIALS
Excel for Beginners
Intermediate Excel
50 Useful Excel Functions
50 More Excel Functions

ACCESS ESSENTIALS
Access for Beginners
Intermediate Access

BUDGETING FOR BEGINNERS
Budgeting for Beginners
Excel for Budgeting

CONTENTS

INTRODUCTION

The purpose of this guide is to introduce you to the basics of using Microsoft PowerPoint. If you've ever found yourself in a situation where you need to present to a larger audience than just a handful of people then you've probably needed PowerPoint. It's great for summarizing and organizing information and also the go-to software for creating presentation slides.

Of course, if you've ever been on the receiving end of a presentation made by a large consulting firm then you've probably seen how PowerPoint can be abused and misused to the point of ridiculousness. (Or is it just me that thinks that crowding a slide with so much information there's no way it could actually be legible if presented on a screen is wrong?)

Anyway. This guide will walk you through the basics of how to use PowerPoint. By the time you finish reading this guide you will be fully capable of creating a basic PowerPoint presentation that includes text, pictures, and/or tables of information. You will also be able to format any text you enter and will know how to add notes to your slides, animate your slides so that each bullet point appears separately, and launch your presentation as a slide show or print a copy or handouts.

(And, yes, this guide will even allow you to create overly-crowded dense slides with too much information on them if that's really what you want to do.)

As you can see, I will also be sprinkling in my opinion throughout this guide so it isn't just going to be how to do things in PowerPoint but why you might want to do it in a certain way.

There are other aspects to PowerPoint that I'm not going to cover in this guide. For example, we're not going to discuss how to use SmartArt.

The goal of this guide is to give you enough information on how to create a basic presentation without overwhelming you with information you may not need. I do, however, end with a discussion of your help options for learning more should you need it.

This guide is written using PowerPoint 2013. If you have a version of PowerPoint prior to 2007 your interface will look very different from mine. At this point, it's probably worth paying to upgrade to a more recent version of Office for anyone using a pre-2007 version, but that's up to you. If you do stick with an older version of PowerPoint, you'll be limited in terms of the resources you can find to help you when you get stuck. (Also the themes that will be discussed in this guide may not exist in your version.)

If you've already read *Word for Beginners* or *Excel for Beginners*, some portions of this guide will be familiar to you because the text options in PowerPoint work much the same way they do in Word and Excel. Also, the PowerPoint interface is structured in much the same way as both Word and Excel. If you're familiar with one of those programs already you should find PowerPoint easier to learn than someone who is new to all three.

Alright then. Now that you know what this guide is going to cover, let's get started with some basics.

BASIC TERMINOLOGY

Before we get started, I want to make sure that we're on the same page in terms of terminology. Some of this will be standard to anyone talking about these programs and some of it is my personal quirky way of saying things, so best to skim through if nothing else.

Tab

I refer to the menu choices at the top of the screen (File, Home, Insert, Design, Transitions, Animations, Slide Show, Review, and View) as tabs. If you click on one you'll see that the way it's highlighted sort of looks like an old-time filing system.

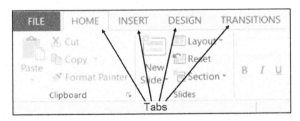

Each tab you select will show you different options. For example, in the image above, I have the Home tab selected and you can do various tasks such as cut/copy/paste, add new slides, change the slide layout, change fonts or font size or font color, change text formatting, add shapes, find/replace, etc. Other tabs give other options.

Click

If I tell you to click on something, that means to use your mouse (or trackpad) to move the arrow on the screen over to a specific location and left-click or right-click on the option. (See the next definition for the difference between left-click and right-click).

If you left-click, this selects the item. If you right-click, this generally creates a dropdown list of options to choose from. If I don't tell you which to do, left- or right-click, then left-click.

Left-click/Right-click

If you look at your mouse or your trackpad, you generally have two flat buttons to press. One is on the left side, one is on the right. If I say left-click that means to press down on the button on the left. If I say right-click that means press down on the button on the right.

Now, as I sadly learned when I had to upgrade computers, not all trackpads have the left- and right-hand buttons. In that case, you'll basically want to press on either the bottom left-hand side of the trackpad or the bottom right-hand side of the trackpad. Since you're working blind it may take a little trial and error to get the option you want working. (Or is that just me?)

Select or Highlight

If I tell you to select text, that means to left-click at the end of the text you want to select, hold that left-click, and move your cursor to the other end of the text you want to select.

Another option is to use the Shift key. Go to one end of the text you want to select. Hold down the shift key and use the arrow keys to move to the other end of the text you want to select. If you arrow up or down, that will select an entire row at a time.

With both methods, which side of the text you start on doesn't matter. You can start at the end and go to the beginning or start at the beginning and go to the end. Just start at one end or the other of the text you want to select.

The text you've selected will then be highlighted in gray.

If you need to select text that isn't touching you can do this by selecting your first section of text and then holding down the Ctrl key and selecting your second section of text using your mouse. (You can't arrow to the second section of text or you'll lose your already selected text.)

Dropdown Menu

If you right-click on a PowerPoint slide, you will see what I'm going to refer to as a dropdown menu. (Sometimes it will actually drop upward if you're towards the bottom of the document.)

A dropdown menu provides you a list of choices to select from like this one that you'll see if you right-click on a Title Slide in a presentation:

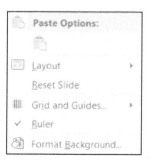

There are also dropdown menus available for some of the options listed under the tabs at the top of the screen. For example, if you go to the Home tab, you'll see small arrows below or next to some of the options, like the Layout option and the Section option in the Slides section. Clicking on those little arrows will give you a dropdown menu with a list of choices to choose from like this one for Layout:

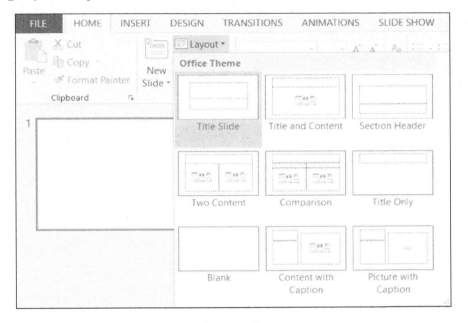

Expansion Arrows

I don't know the official word for these, but you'll also notice at the bottom right corner of most of the sections in each tab that there are little arrows. If you click on one of those arrows PowerPoint will bring up a more detailed set of options, usually through a dialogue box (which we'll discuss next).

In the Home tab, for example, there are expansion arrows for Clipboard, Font, Paragraph, and Drawing. Holding your mouse over the arrow will give a brief description of what clicking on the expansion arrow will do like here for the Clipboard section on the Home tab:

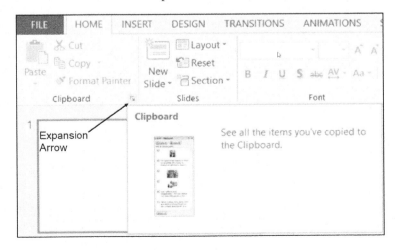

Dialogue Box

Dialogue boxes are pop-up boxes that cover specialized settings. As just mentioned, if you click on an expansion arrow, it will often open a dialogue box that contains more choices than are visible in that section. When you right-click on a PowerPoint content slide and choose Font, Paragraph, or Hyperlink that also opens dialogue boxes.

Dialogue boxes often allow the most granular level of control over an option. For example, this is the Font dialogue box which you can see has more options available than in the Font section of the Home tab.

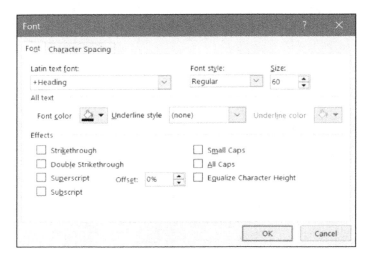

Scroll Bar

PowerPoint has multiple scroll bars that are normally visible. One is on the right-hand side of the slides that are displayed to the left of your screen (but only when there are enough slides to require scrolling). The other is on the right-hand side of the current slide that you're viewing in the main display section of PowerPoint when there are at least two slides in your presentation.

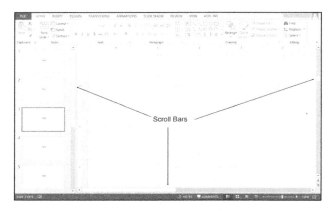

You can either click in the space above or below the scroll bar to move up or down a small amount or you can left-click on the bar, hold the left-click, and drag the bar up or down to move more quickly. You can also use the arrows at the top and the bottom to move up and down through your document.

In the default view where you can see an entire slide in the main screen, the right-hand scroll bar will move you through your presentation. Clicking on the scroll bar for the left-hand pane will keep you on the current slide but show you other slides in the presentation. (That you can then click on if you want to go to that slide.)

I generally use the scroll bar on the left-hand side when I use one at all.

You won't normally see a scroll bar at the bottom of the screen, but it is possible. This would happen if you ever change the zoom level to the point that you're not seeing the entire presentation slide on the screen. (To test this, click on the main slide, go to the View tab, click on Zoom, and choose 400%. You should now see a scroll bar on the bottom of the main section where your current slide is visible.)

Arrow

If I ever tell you to arrow to the left or right or up or down, that just means use your arrow keys. This will move your cursor to the left one space, to the right one space, up one line, or down one line. If you're at the end of a line and arrow to the right, it will take you to the beginning of the next line. If you're at the beginning of a line and arrow to the left, it will take you to the end of the last line.

Cursor

There are two possible meanings for cursor. One is the one I just used. When you're clicked into a PowerPoint slide, you will see that there is a blinking line. This indicates where you are in the document. If you type text, each letter will appear where the cursor was at the time you typed it. The cursor will move (at least in the U.S. and I'd assume most European versions) to the right as you type. This version of the cursor should be visible at all times unless you have text selected.

The other type of cursor is the one that's tied to the movement of your mouse or trackpad. When you're typing, it will not be visible. But stop typing and move your mouse or trackpad, and you'll see it. If the cursor is positioned over your text, it will look somewhat like a tall skinny capital I. If you move it up to the menu options or off to the sides, it becomes a white arrow. (Except for when you position it over any option under the tabs that can be typed in such as Font Size or Font where it will once again look like a skinny capital I.)

Usually I won't refer to your cursor, I'll just say, "click" or "select" or whatever action you need to take with it, and moving the cursor to that location will be implied.

Quick Access Toolbar

In the very top left corner of your screen when you have PowerPoint open you should see a series of symbols. These are part of the Quick Access Toolbar.

You can customize what options appear here by clicking on the downward pointing arrow with a line above it that you see at the very end of the list and then clicking on the commands you want to have available there. (If you don't want a command available, do the same thing. Click on the dropdown arrow and then click on the command so it's no longer selected.) Selected commands have a checkmark next to them.

The Quick Access Toolbar can be useful if there's something you're doing repeatedly that's located on a different tab than something else you're doing repeatedly. I, for example, have customized my toolbar in Word to allow me to easily insert section breaks without having to move away from the Home tab.

To see what command a symbol in your toolbar represents, hold your cursor over the symbol.

Control Shortcuts

Throughout this document, I'm going to mention various control shortcuts that you can use to perform tasks like save, copy, cut, and paste. Each of these will be written as Ctrl + a capital letter, but when you use the shortcut on your computer you don't need to use the capitalized version of the letter. For example, holding down the Ctrl key and the s key at the same time will save your document. I'll write this as Ctrl + S, but that just means hold down the key that says ctrl and the s key at the same time.

Undo

One of the most powerful control shortcuts in PowerPoint (or any program, really) is the Undo option. If you do something you didn't mean to or that you want to take back, use Ctrl + Z to undo it. This should step you back one step and reverse whatever you just did. If you need to reverse more than one step, just keep using Ctrl + Z until you've undone everything you wanted to undo.

(There is also a small left-pointing arrow in the Quick Access Toolbar that will do the same thing.)

ABSOLUTE BASICS

Now let's discuss some absolute basics, like opening, closing, saving, and deleting presentations.

Starting a New PowerPoint Presentation

To start a brand new PowerPoint presentation, I click on PowerPoint 2013 from my applications menu or the shortcut I have on my computer's taskbar. If you're already in PowerPoint and want to open a new PowerPoint presentation you can go to the File tab and choose New from the left-hand menu.

Any of these options will bring up a list of various presentation themes you can choose from. I usually use one of these when I'm doing a non-corporate presentation rather than try to create a presentation from scratch.

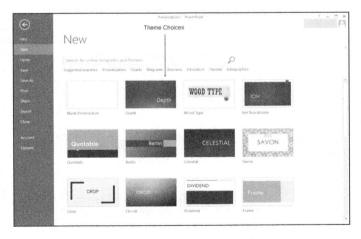

Clicking on any of the themes will bring up a secondary display where you can then use the "More Images" arrows at the bottom to see what the various slides in the presentation will look like. With most of these options you can also click on variant versions that are shown to the right side that are generally the same in terms of layout and font but provide different color options.

For example, the Vapor Trail theme has two options with a black background and two with a white background.

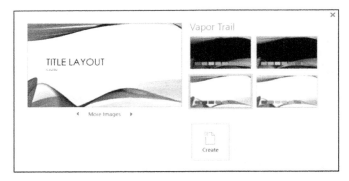

Once you find a template that you like click on Create and PowerPoint will open a new presentation for you that has the Title Slide for that template shown.

As you choose which theme you're going to use, I'd encourage you to think of your potential audience and which presentation is most appropriate for that audience. For example, I personally like the look of Vapor Trail but I would never use it for a presentation to one of my corporate clients. It's too artistic for that audience and the type of consulting I do.

If you have a company-provided template it's best to open that template (discussed next) and work from there.

You can also use Ctrl + N to start a new presentation but that will bring up a Title Slide that has no theme and is just plain white. (You can then choose a theme from the Design tab in PowerPoint as we'll discuss later.)

Opening an Existing PowerPoint File

To open an existing PowerPoint file you can go to the folder where the file is saved and double-click on the file name. Or you can open PowerPoint without selecting a file and it will provide a list of recent documents to choose from on the left-hand side of the screen.

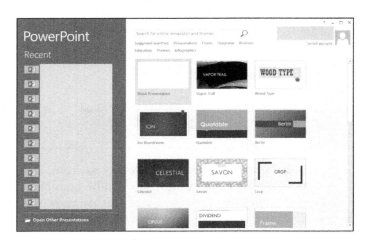

There is also an option at the bottom of that list of recent files to Open Other Presentations. If you click on that it will take you to the Open option that is normally available under the File tab. If you're already in PowerPoint you can access this option by going to the File tab and choosing Open from the left-hand menu or using Ctrl + O.

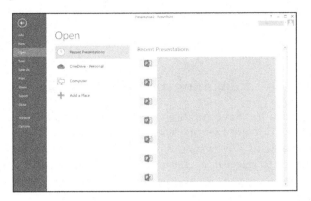

If the document you need is listed, left-click on it once and it will open. (As long as you haven't renamed the file or moved it since it was last opened. In that case, you'll need to navigate to where the file is saved and open it that way, either within PowerPoint or outside of PowerPoint.)

If the document you need is not listed in the list of Recent Presentations or has been moved or renamed since it was last used, click on Computer. (Or OneDrive if you store files in the cloud.) You can then navigate to the folder where the file you need is saved by either clicking on the folder name under Current Folder or Recent Folders (if listed) or by clicking on Browse to bring up the Open dialogue box.

Saving a PowerPoint File

To quickly save your presentation, you can use Ctrl + S or click on the small image of a floppy disk in the top left corner of the screen above File. For a document you've already saved that will overwrite the prior version of the document with the current version and will keep the file name, file type, and file location the same.

If you try to save a file that has never been saved before, it will automatically default to the Save As option which requires that you specify where to save the file, give it a name, and designate the file type. There are defaults for name and format, but you'll want to change the name of the document to something better than Document2.

You can also choose Save As when you want to change the location of a file, the name of a file, or the file type. (With respect to file type, I sometimes need to, for example, save a presentation file as a .pdf file or a .jpg file instead.) To do so, go to File and choose Save As from there.

The first choice you have to make for Save As is where you want to save the file. I see a list of my most recent seven folders listed and can also choose to Browse if I want to use a different location than one of the folders listed.

When you click on the location where you want to save the file, this will bring up the Save As dialogue box. Type in the name you want for the file and choose the file type. My file type defaults to PowerPoint Presentation (.pptx), but that can be changed using the dropdown next to "Save as type."

If you had already saved the file and you choose to Save As but keep the same location, name, and format as before, PowerPoint will overwrite the previous version of the file just like it would have if you'd used Save.

If you just want to rename a file, it's actually best to close the file and then go to where the file is saved and rename it that way rather than use Save As. Using Save As will keep the original of the file as well as creating the newer version. That's great when you want version control (which is rarely needed for PowerPoint), but not when you just wanted to rename your file from Great Presentation v22 to Great Presentation FINAL.

Renaming a PowerPoint File

As discussed above, you can use Save As to give an existing file a new name, but that approach will leave you with two versions of the file, one with the old name and one with the new name. If you just want to change the name of the existing file, close it and then navigate to where you've saved it. Click on the file name once to select it, click on it a second time to highlight the name, and then type in the new name you want to use, replacing the old one. If you rename the file this way outside of PowerPoint, there will only be one version of the file left, the one with the new name you wanted.

Just be aware that if you rename a file by navigating to where it's located and changing the name you won't be able to access the file from the Recent Presentations list under Open since that will still list the old name which no longer exists.

Deleting a PowerPoint File

You can't delete a PowerPoint file from within PowerPoint. You need to close the file you want to delete and then navigate to where the file is stored and delete the file there without opening it. Once you've located the file, click on the file name. (Only enough to select it. Make sure you haven't double-clicked and highlighted the name which will delete the file name but not the file.) Next, choose Delete from the menu at the top of the screen, or right-click and choose Delete from the dropdown menu.

Closing a PowerPoint File

To close a PowerPoint file click on the X in the top right corner or go to File and then choose Close. (You can also use Ctrl + W, but I never have.)

If no changes have been made to the document since you saved it last, it will just close.

If changes have been made, PowerPoint should ask you if you want to save those changes. You can either choose to save them, not save them, or cancel closing the document and leave it open. I almost always default to saving any changes. If I'm in doubt about whether I'd be overwriting something important, I cancel and choose to Save As and save the current file as a later version of the document just in case (e.g., Great Presentation v2).

If you had copied an image or a large block of text, you may also have a box pop up asking if you want to keep that image or text when you close the document. Usually the answer to this is no, but if you had planned on pasting that image or text somewhere else and hadn't yet done so, you can say to keep it on the clipboard.

YOUR WORKSPACE

Whether you choose to start a brand new file or open an existing file, you'll end up in the main workspace for PowerPoint. It looks something like this:

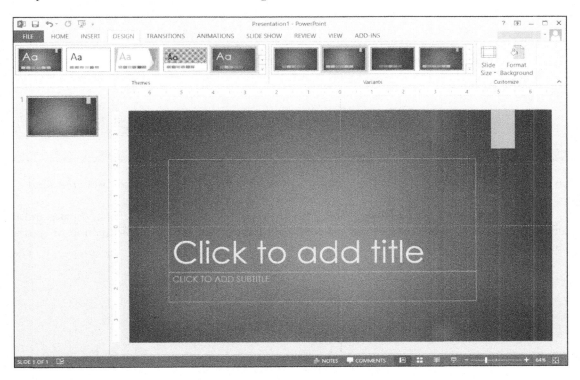

We'll walk through this in more detail in the *Working with Your Presentation Slides* section but I just wanted you to see right now that there's a left-hand pane that shows all of the slides in the presentation and then a main section of the screen that shows the slide you're currently working on.

For a new presentation there's just the one slide.

* * *

For a fully-built presentation, it will look more like this:

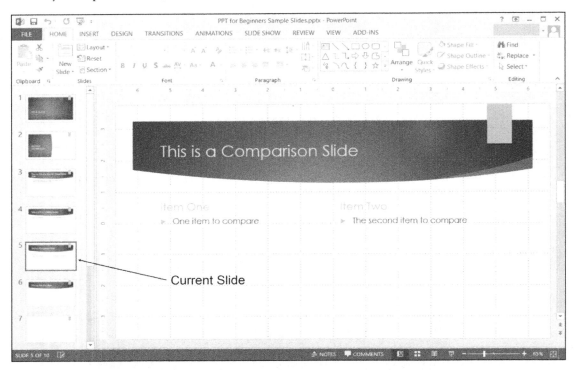

The slide you're currently seeing in the main section of the screen will have a dark border around it in the left-hand pane and your slides will be numbered starting at 1.

Across the top are your menu tabs and there are scroll bars for both the left-hand pane and the main section as well. Along the bottom are a couple of additional pieces of information or settings, including a zoom option in the bottom right corner.

CHOOSING A
PRESENTATION THEME

If you use Ctrl + N to start a new presentation you will have a blank presentation with no design elements. As a beginner, I would suggest that you use one of the PowerPoint designs for your presentation rather than create a design from scratch. (And the rest of this guide assumes that's the choice you're going to make. I do not cover in this guide how to build a presentation from scratch. That's intermediate-level.)

Also, sometimes you're going to choose a theme when you start a new presentation and then decide that that design doesn't work for your purposes and want to change it.

It's very easy to switch between design themes in PowerPoint, so let's walk through how to do it.

Open the presentation you want to change.

Go to the Design tab.

You should see that the Themes section takes up most of the screen.

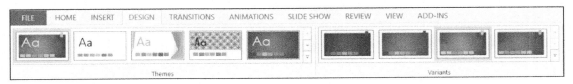

The far left-hand thumbnail in that section is your current design template.

On the right-hand side of the Design tab you'll see a separate section titled Variants.

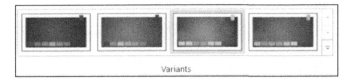

This will show different color variations on your current theme. So with the Ion theme if I wanted a purple background instead of a blue one, I could click on that image in the Variant section to change my presentation.

The rest of the thumbnails in the Themes section are other design templates you can choose from.

I would recommend having a Title and Content Slide visible in your presentation and using that to decide. (Right-click in the left-hand pane and choose New Slide to add one.) The reason for this is that some of the design templates put the header section of the slide at the bottom instead of the top. Or they have a colored background on all of the slides instead of just the Title Slide. You'll want to know that before you choose that theme since it can significantly impact the effectiveness of your presentation.

(My recommendation would be to choose a theme with a white background for the main slides and with the title section at the top. At least for standard corporate presentations.)

To see what your slides will look like before you change the theme, just hold your cursor over each thumbnail image in the Theme section of the Design tab and the slide in the main screen will change to show that theme.

To select that theme, click on the thumbnail image. All of your slides should then change over to the new theme and that thumbnail should now be visible as the left-most thumbnail in the Theme section.

(If you are using sections in your presentation, something we won't cover in this guide, then only the slides in your current section will change to the new theme. So using sections would be a way to use multiple themes in a single presentation, although I wouldn't recommend doing that. The point of using a design theme is that it provides cohesiveness to a presentation.)

POWERPOINT SLIDE TYPES

There are a number of slide types available to you in PowerPoint. Probably more than you'll actually need. But I wanted to run through them real quick before we go any further because I'm going to occasionally refer to a slide type and I want you to know what I'm talking about when I do so.

The images below use the Ion Boardroom theme. If you want to change the slide type of a slide, you can right-click on that slide, go to Layout, and choose from the listed options there. Not all themes or templates will have all slide types in them. And different themes may have the elements in different locations on the slide. For example, some put the header at the bottom instead of the top.

You can put together a perfectly adequate presentation with just the Title Slide, Section Header, and Title and Content slide types, but I'll walk through most of the others for you just in case.

Title Slide

The Title slide is the default first slide for a presentation. It has a section for adding a title and a subtitle and, if you choose one of the templates provided in PowerPoint, a background that covers the rest of the slide and matches your chosen theme.

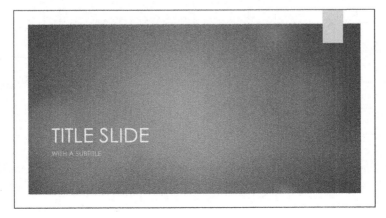

Section Header

If you are going to have sections within your presentation, then you'll want to separate them using a Section Header slide. Like the title slides above this slide will have a colored background that matches your theme. It will generally have the text in a different position or using a different font or font size to distinguish it from the title slide or will use a different color for the background or move the background image to a new location.

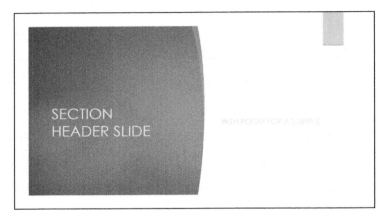

Title and Content Slide

The Title and Content slide is the one I use for most of my presentations. It has a section where you can describe what the slide is discussing and then a content box where you can add text, images, etc. When you're doing a basic presentation with a bulleted set of talking points, this is the slide that you'll probably use the most often.

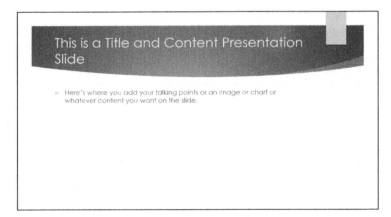

While most themes will have the title portion at the top (and I think that's the best choice for a corporate presentation) some of the themes have the title portion at the bottom or off to the side, so check your theme before you choose it. For example, this is the Title and Content Slide from the Slice theme using the exact same text as the image above.

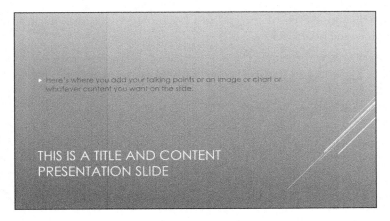

As you can also see above, content slides will sometimes have a colored background and sometimes will not depending on the theme you choose. Also, some themes use all caps in the title section and some do not. If you're switching between themes, be careful with this because it's easy with a theme that uses all caps to not pay attention to your capitalization and then move to a theme that uses upper and lower case and have some words capitalized and some not.

Two Content

The Two Content slide is another content slide. This slide has a section for a title and then two content boxes. It can be a good choice for when you want to either have two separate bulleted lists side by side or when you want to have text next to an image. You put the text in one of the boxes and the image in the other.

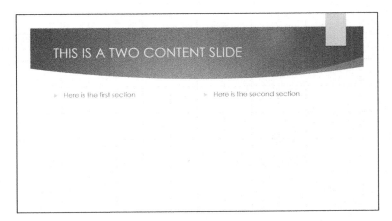

Comparison

The Comparison slide is also a content slide. It's much like the Two Content slide except it has added sections directly above each of the two text boxes where you can put header text to describe the contents of each of the boxes below.

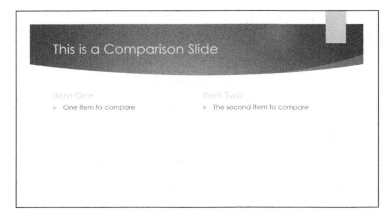

Title Only

The Title Only slide is a content slide that just has the title section and nothing else below it. You can add elements to the body of this slide, such as a text box or an image, but there is no pre-defined space for it like with the prior content slide types. It will have the same background as content slides for your selected theme.

Content With Caption

The Content With Caption slide is another content slide. In this one the title section covers half of the screen and there are two text boxes where you can add text, images, etc. One is below the title and the other takes up the other side of the slide.

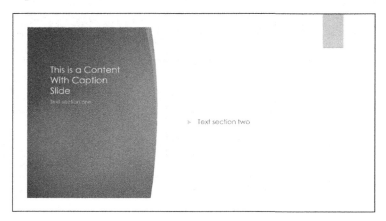

Picture With Caption

The Picture With Caption slide is a slide you'd probably use for an appendix or some information you're calling out separate from the main presentation. It has a large section for a picture and then a section for title and text. (In the picture below I added a stock photo of some keyboard keys to the section for the photo and it took a portion of the image and scaled it to fit.)

Quote With Caption

The Quote With Caption slide is a slide that has quote marks around the main text section and then a smaller text box for an attribution of who said the quote as well as a larger text box for comments.

Blank

The blank slide has the same background as the other content slides for your chosen theme, but nothing else.

Other

Some themes will have even more pre-formatted slide types you can use. The Ion Boardroom theme has a three-column version as well as a few others I didn't cover here. And some won't have this many. If you need a specific slide type, be sure to check that that slide type is available before you get too far into working with your chosen theme.

WORKING WITH YOUR PRESENTATION SLIDES

In this chapter we're going to assume that you've created a brand new presentation using one of the templates. So now you find yourself in PowerPoint with a title slide visible on the left-hand side and in the main screen:

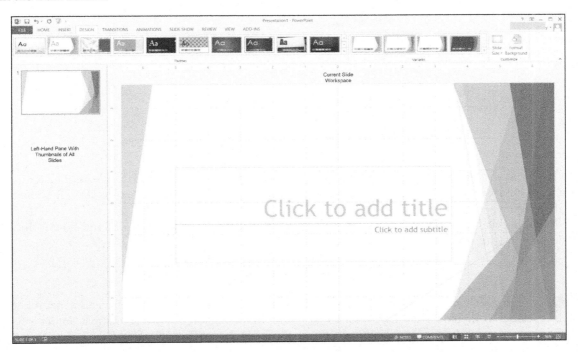

First things first, let's talk about what you're seeing. On the left-hand side of the screen are thumbnail (i.e., small) images of your slides. As you add new slides to your presentation they'll appear in this left-hand pane. In the center of the screen and taking up most of the space is the current slide you are working on. Because there's only this one slide to begin with it's going to be your title slide when you first open the file.

You can click on any of the slides in the left-hand pane or you can click on the slide in the center. Depending on which one you're clicked into, you'll be able to do different things such as add text to a slide or move a slide to a different location.

Let's start with the left-hand pane because that's where you'll work to change the positioning of your slides as well as add new ones or delete ones you no longer want.

If you right-click into the blank space below the title slide, you'll see that you have the option to add a new slide or add a new section. (In the hundreds of presentations I've done I've never needed to use sections so we're going to set that aside as an intermediate topic.) If you had copied slides from another presentation or even this one, you could also paste them as well, but since we haven't copied any slides yet that's not actually an available option. So all you have is the New Slide option.

If you choose that option, PowerPoint will insert a Title and Content slide for you. (Since this is the most common slide type I use for inputting information, it's convenient that PowerPoint defaults to that slide type.)

Now that we have two slides, let's discuss how you can select a slide or slides and how to move slides within your presentation.

Selecting a Slide or Slides

To select a single slide, you simply left-click on the slide where it's visible in the left-hand pane. When a slide is selected it should have a darker border around it. In my version of PowerPoint that border is red.

If you want to select more than once slide, you can select the first slide and then hold down the Ctrl key as you left-click on the next slide or slides that you want to select. When you do this each slide you click on will have that dark border around it.

Slides do not need to be next to one another for you to select them this way.

If you have a range of slides that you want to select, you can use the Shift key instead. Click on the slide at the top or the bottom of the range of slides you want, hold down the Shift key, and then click on the slide at the other end of the range of slides you want. All slides within that range, including the first slide you clicked and the second slide you clicked, should now have a dark border around them.

So, for example, if I want to select the first four slides in my presentation, I can click on the first slide, hold down the Shift key, and then click on the fourth slide. Or I could click on the fourth slide, hold down the Shift key, and then click on the first slide. As long as the slides you click on are at the beginning and end of your range of desired slides, you will select all of them.

(You can also combine methods of selecting slides to, for example, select a range of slides using Shift and then select an additional slide using the Ctrl key.)

No matter how many slides you select, the main screen will only show one of them.

To remove your selection of multiple slides, click in the gray area around any of the slides or on the main presentation slide.

Moving a Slide or Slides

The easiest way to move a slide or slides to a different position within your presentation is to select the slide(s) (as noted above) and then left-click and drag the slide(s) to the new location. As you move your chosen slide(s) you'll see the slides in the left-hand pane moving upward or downward to leave a space for your slides to be inserted. (It sounds weird, but just try it and you'll see what I'm talking about.)

If you've selected more than one slide, you can left-click on any of the slides you've selected and drag and all of the slides will move to the new location even if they weren't next to one another before.

Cutting a Slide or Slides

If you right-click on a slide or slides that you've selected and choose Cut from the dropdown menu, you can remove the slide or slides from their current location in the presentation. You can also do this by selecting the slide(s) and then using Ctrl + X.

Where cutting differs from deleting, which will have the same effect of removing the slides, is that cutting the slides allows you to move them elsewhere. You could cut them and then paste them into another location in that same presentation (using Paste which we'll discuss in a moment) or you could paste them into another PowerPoint presentation.

Cutting only deletes slides if you cut them and then choose not to put them in a new location.

Usually you can just select and drag slides into a new location within your presentation as we just discussed above, but if you have a very long presentation (say 200 slides) and want to move a slide from the beginning to the end, for example, it can be faster to cut the slide, scroll down to the end, and then paste.

You can also cut a slide by clicking on it, going to the Clipboard section of the Home tab, and choosing Cut from there.

Copying a Slide or Slides

If you right-click on a slide or slides that you've selected and choose Copy from the dropdown men, you can keep a version of the slides exactly where they were while creating a copy of those slides that you can then move into a new presentation or move to a new location within your existing presentation. (Using Paste which we'll discuss next.)

You can also use Ctrl + C to copy a set of slides. So select the slides you want to copy and then type Ctrl + C.

Where copy differs from cut is that it leaves the original version of the slides where they were. You now end up with two identical copies of that set of slides and you can place that second copy of the slides wherever you need them, either in your current presentation or another one.

(I tend to use Duplicate Slide instead when I'm working in a presentation. We'll talk about that one in a moment.)

You can also copy a slide by clicking on it, going to the Clipboard section of the Home tab, and choosing Copy from there.

Pasting a Slide or Slides

If you copy or cut a slide or slides and want to use them elsewhere, you need to paste them into that new location. You can do a basic paste by clicking into the space where you want to put those slides (so between two existing slides or in the gray space at the end of the presentation, for example) and using Ctrl + V.

If you are clicked onto a slide when you paste, your copied or cut slides will be pasted in below that slide.

You can also right-click where you want to paste a slide and choose from the paste options.

The first option, which has a small a in the bottom right corner, is Use Destination Theme. If you're cutting or copying and pasting within an existing presentation this won't mean much. But I've used this one often when working with a corporate PowerPoint template where someone drafted a presentation without using the corporate template and then handed it off to me and asked me to make it look like it should. (Always a pleasure when that happens.)

In those cases, I copy all of the slides from the version of the presentation I've been given and paste it into the corporate template using the destination theme option. This will convert the slides you pasted in from whatever theme they were using to your corporate template theme.

(You can test this for yourself by cutting a slide from your current presentation, changing the theme of your current presentation, and then right-clicking and pasting the slide back into your presentation using the Use Destination Theme option.)

Use Destination Theme is also what happens when you just use Ctrl + V.

The second paste option you have, the one with the paintbrush in the bottom right corner, is Keep Source Formatting. This does what it says, it keeps the formatting the slide(s) already had. Sometimes it's important to do this especially if you've done a lot of custom work on a slide and don't want your images, charts, etc. resized when you move them into a new presentation.

The third paste option, the one with a photo icon in the bottom right corner, is to paste a slide in as a Picture. That means the slide can no longer be edited. It's like someone took a snapshot of that slide and now you just have that snapshot. If you try to use this option with multiple slides only the first slide will paste in.

I would expect you won't use this one often.

You can also paste slides by going to the Clipboard section of the Home tab and choosing Paste from there. The more advanced options are available by clicking on the arrow under Paste.

Adding a New Slide

If you right-click on an existing slide in the presentation or in the gray area in the left-hand pane, you can add a new slide by choosing New Slide from the dropdown menu.

If you click on a slide and then choose New Slide, the slide that is added to your presentation will match the type of the slide you were clicked onto when you made that choice.

If you click in the gray area to add a slide, the slide type will match the slide directly above where you had clicked. (With the exception of a Title slide. In that case the new slide added will be a Title and Content slide.)

You can also go to the Slides section of the Home tab and click on New Slide there. If you use the dropdown arrow next to New Slide you can choose the layout for the new slide before you add it.

Duplicating a Slide

If you want to create a duplicate of an existing slide (something I do when I've created custom formatting and don't want to have to recreate it on each slide), you can right-click on a slide and choose Duplicate Slide. This will create an exact duplicate of the slide you right-clicked on.

You can also duplicate a slide by clicking on the slide, going to the Clipboard section of the Home tab, clicking on the arrow next to Copy, and choosing Duplicate from the dropdown menu.

Deleting a Slide

To delete a slide, you can click on that slide and then hit the Delete or Backspace key. Either one will work. Or you can right-click on that slide and choose Delete Slide from the dropdown menu.

Choosing the Slide Layout

To change the type of slide, select the slide or slides you need to change, right-click, go to Layout, and select the type you want from the available options. Each one will have the type listed as well as a small thumbnail image.

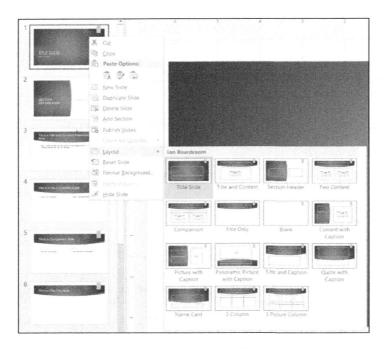

Different themes will have different options available. For example, the Ion theme has a Quote with Caption slide option that is not available in the Integral theme.

If you're using a custom theme (such as a corporate one) and don't have example slides in the presentation of the type you need, you may not have that layout option available to choose even though it exists in your corporate template. (This is why if I'm ever working with a corporate template I leave the sample slides in my presentation until I'm done and then delete them at the very last minute to make sure I won't need one of those choices.)

PowerPoint will do its best to change your current slide over to the chosen layout, but if you already had content in a slide when you changed the layout be sure to review each slide to make sure the way that PowerPoint changed the slide to the new layout makes sense.

You can also select a slide or slides, go to the Slides section of the Home tab, click on the dropdown arrow next to Layout, and choose your layout from there.

Resetting a Slide

If you makes changes to the layout of a slide, by for example changing the size of the text boxes or their location, and want to go back to the original layout for that slide type, you can right-click on the slide and choose Reset Slide from the dropdown menu. According to PowerPoint, this will "reset the position, size, and formatting of the slide placeholders to their default settings."

You can also click on a slide and go to the Slides section of the Home tab and choose Reset from there.

ADDING TEXT TO A PRESENTATION SLIDE

Now let's turn our attention from the left-hand pane to the main section of your PowerPoint screen where your current slide is shown.

Adding text to an existing slide is very simple. You click and type.

For example, here, is a Title slide:

You can see that the slide says "CLICK TO ADD TITLE" and "CLICK TO ADD SUBTITLE". And it's almost that easy. Click on where it say that and type. Click away when you're done. You will now be able to see whatever text you typed in that space and formatted according to that theme. (Usually that will cover text color and whether the text appears in all caps or not.)

If you add a different type of slide, such as a Title and Content slide, you'll see that that slide also has sections for adding text. It says "CLICK TO ADD TITLE" and "CLICK TO ADD TEXT". Many of the themes are pre-formatted to create bulleted lists that match the theme. As soon as you type, your text will be shown as part of a bulleted list. And each time you hit Enter a new bullet point will appear.

This is a Title and Content Presentation Slide

- Here's where you add your talking points or an image or chart or whatever content you want on the slide.
- And here's a second point.
- And another one.

If you need to create subpoints, use the tab key to indent the line before you start typing your text. In some templates this will also change the type of bullet used or change the size of the bullet.

If you need to remove an indent, use Shift+Tab before your start typing.

- **And another one.**
  - *Tab before typing to indent, note the different bullet point style*
  - *And then just hit Enter*
- **Shift + Tab before typing to remove the indent**

For lines that have already been added where you need to adjust the indent, click to the left of the first letter in that line and then use Tab or Shift + Tab to adjust the indent. You can also use the Decrease List Level and Increase List Level options in the Paragraph section of the Home tab. They're the ones with lines with an arrow pointing either left or right in the middle of the top row.

By default the PowerPoint themes use fonts and font sizes that are legible for a presentation given on a projector. But the slides are also dynamic in the sense that as you add more and more and more to a slide the text in that slide will adjust in size to fit in the text box on the slide. Be careful with this.

For two reasons. First, if you let the font size get too small, no one will be able to read your slide. Why put together a presentation that no one can read?

Second, because this can happen on a slide-by-slide basis it can create a disjointed presentation. If one slide has bullet points in a 20 point size and another has bullet points in a 14 point size and another has them in an 11 point size, even if the font and colors are consistent across slides it can be jarring.

I try when I can to make the font size consistent across slides. So if I do have a very busy slide that requires a smaller font size than the default, then I'll usually change all other slides in the presentation to match that font size. (Easier to simplify the language instead, but that's not always an option when working on group projects.)

Be especially careful about legibility with respect to your subpoints. Each level of subpoint generally uses a smaller font size than the last. It's easy to get to the point where the last level can't be read. I'd advise limiting your bulleted lists to three levels at most and ideally just two levels to avoid this issue.

(A good template will limit this. So, for example, the Ion Boardroom theme stops decreasing font size when the font size reaches 12 point.)

* * *

If you need to cut, copy, or paste text from within a slide, it works much the same way as it did for the slides in the left-hand pane.

To cut text, highlight the text you want to cut and then use Ctrl + X or go to the Clipboard section of the Home tab and choose Cut from there. You can also right-click and choose Cut from the dropdown menu.

As you'll recall, cutting text removes it from its current location but still allows you to paste that text elsewhere.

To copy text, highlight the text you want to copy and then use Ctrl + C or to go to the Clipboard section of the Home tab and choose Copy from there. You can also right-click and choose Copy from the dropdown menu.

Copying keeps the text in its current location but also allows you to paste that text elsewhere.

To paste text, click on the location where you want to place the text you copied or cut and then use Ctrl + V. If you paste text this way it will take on the formatting of the location where you paste it. Your other options are to click where you want to paste the text and then go to the Clipboard section of the Home tab and click on the arrow under Paste or right-click.

This will give you the Paste Options list of choices:

The option with the lower case a in the bottom right corner will use the formatting of the location where you are pasting your text.

The option with the paintbrush in the bottom right corner will keep the formatting the text already had.

The option with the small picture in the bottom right corner will paste the selected text in as an image. (You will not be able to edit this text after it's pasted because it will no longer be considered text.)

The option with the large A in the bottom right corner, will paste as text only. (This should generally have the same result as pasting with the destination theme, the first option.)

(There are more specialized paste options available under the Clipboard option, but for a beginner level I don't think they're worth discussing here. If you want to look at them click on Paste Special from the dropdown.)

* * *

If you need to remove text you can either cut that text or you can use the Delete or Backspace keys. Backspace will delete text to the left of the cursor. Delete will delete text to the right of the cursor.

If you've highlighted the text you want to delete then either one will work.

Delete and Backspace can also delete bullet points or the numbers or letters in a numbered list.

FORMATTING TEXT IN A PRESENTATION

All of the templates include text that's of a pre-defined size and using a pre-selected font. If you can stick to the defaults, your life will be much easier because then you can simply add a new slide and everything will be all set to work together.

But it's quite possible that at some point in time you'll want to customize a font size or change the font used or maybe even the color of the font. So in this section we'll walk through how to do that. Just know that doing so will add complications to your life.

As soon as you type text into a presentation slide you should see that the Font section of the Home tab is not only visible but populated with values. (Before you add text it will be visible but grayed out.)

Let's walk through what you can do using these options. For each option, you need to have selected the text you want to edit before you make your choice.

Font

The top left option in the Font section is where you select the font for your presentation. The current font will be visible in the dropdown box.

If you want to change that font you can click on the dropdown arrow and choose from the list of available fonts. The list will show the theme fonts first, your recently used fonts next, and then all available fonts in alphabetical order.

If you start typing a font name that will take you to that portion of the alphabetical listing. So typing T in the white space shows Tahoma and takes me to the T section of the font listing.

For a font that's later in the alphabet, it's often easier to start typing the name, but there is a scroll bar on the right-hand side of the listing that you can use to move through your selections.

The name of the fonts are written in that font to give you an idea of what each font will look like when used.

Another option is to right-click on your text to bring up what I call the mini-formatting bar. It has a font dropdown menu just like the one on the Home tab that you can use to change the font.

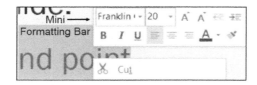

Or you can right-click on your text, choose Font from the dropdown menu, and then change the Latin Text Font box in the Font dialogue box to the font you want using the dropdown to select your font and then clicking on OK.

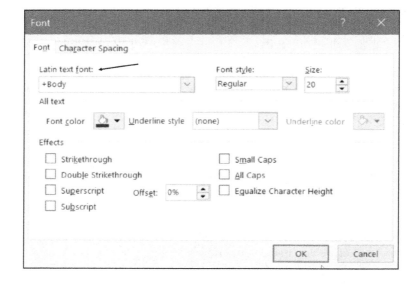

Font Size

The next option in the Font section of the Home tab is your font size. This determines how big the text is on the slide. 36 point is a good visible size for headers. 24 or 18 point is a good size for your main body text but you could probably go as small as 12 point. If you're doing handouts instead of a presentation, you can use 8 or 10 point for footnotes. Don't go smaller than that.

You have a number of options for changing your font size.

The first is to click into the box with the current font size and type a new value.

You can also click on the dropdown arrow next to the current font size and choose from one of the values in the dropdown.

Or you can use the Increase Font Size and Decrease Font Size options that are next to the font size dropdown menu and look like the letter A with either an up or a down arrow in the top right corner. If you use the increase and decrease font size options, the only values available to you are the ones in the dropdown menu.

You can also right-click and use the mini-formatting toolbar or right-click and choose Font from the dropdown menu and then change the font size in the Font dialogue box.

There are also control shortcuts for changing the font size upward or downward one level, but I honestly don't recommend learning them because I don't think you'll need them often enough to make it worthwhile. They are Ctrl + Shift + > to increase one font size and Ctrl + Shift + < to decrease one font size.

Font Color

The option in the bottom right corner of the Font section that looks like an A with a red line under it (at least when you first open PowerPoint—the line color can change as you work in PowerPoint) is where you can change the color of your text.

Click on the dropdown arrow and you'll see seventy different colors you can choose from.

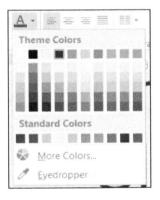

If you need a different or a custom color, click on More Colors. This will bring up the Colors dialogue box. On the Standard tab you can choose from the honeycomb of colors available by clicking on any of the colored squares. On the Custom tab you can input your own RGB values or HSL values. You can also click into the rainbow of colors above that or move the slider for different shades of a color. The color you've selected will show under New in the bottom right corner of the Colors dialogue box.

Another option available to you in PowerPoint is the eyedropper. When you click on the dropdown arrow for Font Color the bottom option in that list is the Eyedropper Text Fill. If you click on this and then click on a color in one of your presentation slides, PowerPoint will grab that color you clicked on. It will then be shown as a color you can use under Recent Colors in the color dropdown menu.

(I use the eyedropper often to pull a color from one of my book covers when I'm creating a related presentation. I import the cover, pull the color from it using the eyedropper, and then delete the cover.)

All of these color options are also available by right-clicking to pull up the mini-formatting bar.

You can also right-click, go to Font in the dropdown menu, and then on the Font tab of the Font dialogue box choose a font color from there. (The Font dialogue box dropdown does not, however, include the eyedropper option.)

Bolding Text

To bold text, highlight your text and click on the capital B on the left-hand side of the second row in the Font section of the Home tab.

You can also right-click on your selected text and click on the capital B in the mini-formatting bar.

Or you can use Ctrl + B after you've selected your text.

Or can right-click, choose Font from the dropdown menu, and then change the Font Style in the Font dialogue box to Bold. Or Bold Italic if you want both bold and italic.

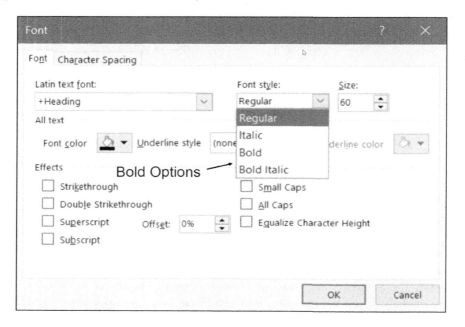

To remove bolding from text, select the text and either click on the capital B or use Ctrl + B once more. If you select text that is partially bolded and partially not bolded, you will need to do this twice because the first time will apply bolding to the entire selection and the second time will remove it from the entire selection.

You can also select your text, right-click, choose Font from the dropdown menu, and then change the Font Style to Regular.

Italicizing Text

To italicize text, select your text and click on the slanted I on the left-hand side of the second row in the Font section.

You can also click on the slanted I in the mini-formatting bar.

Or you can use Ctrl + I.

Or you can right-click, choose Font from the dropdown menu, and then change the Font Style in the Font dialogue box to Italic. (Or Bold Italic if you want both bold and italic.)

To remove italics from text, select the text and either click on the slanted I or use Ctrl + I once more. If you select text that is partially italicized and partially not, you will need to do this twice because the first time will apply italics to the entire selection and the second time will remove it from the entire selection.

You can also just right-click, choose Font from the dropdown menu, and then change the Font Style in the Font dialogue box to Regular.

Underlining Text

To underline text, click on the capital U with a line under it on the left-hand side of the second row in the Font section.

You can also click on the capital U with a line under it in the mini-formatting bar.

Or you can use Ctrl + U.

Or you can right-click, select Font from the dropdown menu, go to the Font dialogue box and choose from the dropdown menu next to Underline Style.

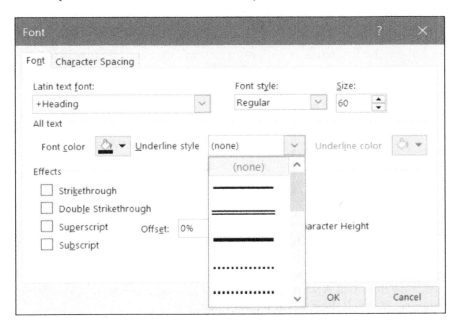

To remove underlining from text, select the text and either click on the capital U with a line under it or use Ctrl + U once more. If you select text that is partially underlined and partially not, you will need to do this twice because the first time will apply underlining to the entire selection and the second time will remove it from the entire selection.

You can also go to the Font dialogue box and change the Underline Style to (none).

If you want a different underline style than just the basic single line underline, it's best to use the Font dialogue box. (So right-click and choose Font from the dropdown menu and then change the Underline Style.) There you'll have the choice of a double-line or a bolder line than standard as well as dotted lines and wavy lines in various styles. (Don't get carried away here. Remember, clean and simple is better than fancy and complicated when trying to convey information to other people.)

To remove a non-standard underline, select the text and use Ctrl + U or click on the U in the Font section until there is no underline remaining. It will usually take two tries, because the first time will convert it to a standard underline. You can also just go back to the Font dialogue box and change the underline style back to none.

Change Case

If you want your text to be in all caps or if you have text that is already in all caps that you want to have in normal case, then you will need to change the case of that text.

You can do this in the Font section of the Home tab by clicking on the arrow next to the Aa in the bottom row on the right-hand side. This will give you a dropdown menu with choices for sentence case, lower case, upper case, capitalize each word, and toggle case.

Sentence case will capitalize the first letter of the first word in each sentence or text string.

Lower case will put all of the letters in lower case.

Upper case will put all of the letters in upper case.

Capitalize each word will capitalize the first letter of each word.

Toggle case will put the first letter of each word in lower case and all other letters in upper case.

Clear Text Formatting

If you've edited a text selection and want to return it to the default for that theme, you can select the text and then click on the small A with an eraser in the top right corner of the Font section. (If you hold your mouse over it, it will show as Clear All Formatting.)

This will change the selection to whatever font, font size, and font formatting would be appropriate for that location within that theme. It does not change the case of the letters but it will revert the font, font color, font size, and any bold, italics or underline back to the default for the theme.

Other

You'll note that there were a few other options available in the Font section of the Home tab (text shadowing, strikethrough, and character spacing) as well as additional options in the Font dialogue box.

I've chosen not to cover them here because I want to keep this guide focused on a basic level of PowerPoint presentation and those are ones I expect you wouldn't use often, but if there's a text effect you want to apply in a PowerPoint slide that I didn't cover, the Font section of the Home tab or right-clicking and choosing Font to bring up the Font dialogue box are a good place to start.

For more advanced text formatting you'll want to look to the Format tab under Drawing Tools that will appear when you click on any text in your presentation. That's intermediate level so we're not going to cover it here.

Next let's talk about paragraph-level formatting.

FORMATTING PARAGRAPHS IN A PRESENTATION

What we just talked about are formatting changes that you can make at the word level. But there are other changes you can make at the paragraph level. These are generally covered in the Paragraph section of the Home tab but some of them are also available in the mini formatting bar or by right-clicking and choosing Paragraph from the dropdown menu.

With the paragraph formatting options you don't have to highlight all of the text, you just need to be clicked onto the line or into the section you want to change. Let's start with one we already covered earlier, Decrease List Level and Increase List Level.

Decrease List Level/Increase List Level

A lot of PowerPoint presentations rely on using bulleted lists. And when you use a bulleted list you will often want to either indent the next line or decrease the indent of the next line.

To indent the next line, you can either click at the beginning of the line and use the Tab key. Or you can click anywhere on the line and use the Increase List Level option in the Paragraph section of the Home tab.

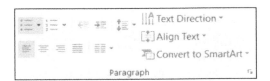

This is the one with a right-pointing arrow embedded in a series of lines that is on the top row and towards the middle on the left-hand side.

To decrease the indent on the next line, you can either click at the beginning of the line and use Shift + Tab (so hold down the Shift key and then the Tab key) or you can click anywhere on the line and use the Decease List Level option in the Paragraph section of the Home tab. This is the one with a left-pointing arrow embedded in a series of lines that is on the top row and also towards the middle on the left-hand side.

If the decrease list level option is grayed out (like it is in the picture above) that's because you're already at the far left-hand side and can't decrease the indent any further.

These options may or may not be available with plain text that isn't already bulleted or numbered. It will depend on where the text is located within the presentation slide.

Left-Align/Center/Right-Align a Paragraph

Your next option is to change the alignment of the text in your paragraph.

You have four options. You can have left-aligned text, meaning that each new line starts along the left-hand side of the text box. You can have centered text, meaning each line is centered within the text box. You can have right-aligned text, meaning each line ends along the right-hand side of the text box. Or you can have justified text meaning your text will be spread out across the text box so that it's even on both the right-hand edge and the left-hand edge.

All of this occurs within a single text box. If you look closely at the slide formats you'll see that each section with a "Click to add text" or similar message is within a box with a dotted line border. This is a text box. So any changes you make to your text to align it will be made not with respect to the entire PowerPoint slide but instead with respect to the boundaries of that specific text box.

Here are examples of all four options using a text box that has the same dimensions.

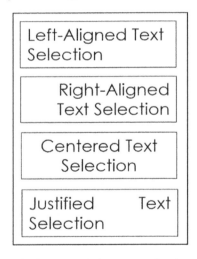

Depending on where your text is and what type it is, your selection will either apply to just the line of text you're clicked onto or all of the contents of the text box. So you may have to do some fiddling around to get the text aligned the way you want it. If you highlight rows of text and then make your alignment choice, all of the rows will change at once.

You can also right-click, choose Paragraph from the dropdown menu, and then choose your alignment option from Alignment dropdown menu in the General section of the Paragraph dialogue box. That also gives you the option to have distributed text.

Top/Middle/Bottom Align Text

You can also align text within a text box along the top, middle, or bottom of that text box. To choose which alignment option you want, go to the Paragraph section of the Home tab and click on the arrow next to Align Text in the middle on the right-hand side of the section.

Choose the option you want from the dropdown menu. Top-aligned text will have the first row at the top of the text box. Bottom-aligned text will have the last row at the bottom of the text box. Middle-aligned text will have the rows of text centered between the top and bottom of the text box

Top Align		
	Middle Align	
		Bottom Align

Your choice will apply to all text within the text box.

Using Multiple Columns

If you want your text displayed on a slide in multiple columns you have two choices. First, you can choose a slide layout that has two equally sized sections like the Two Content slide format and then input your text into both of those boxes, split evenly across the two boxes.

Or you can use the multiple column formatting option. To split a column into multiple columns, simply click anywhere within that column and then go to the Paragraph section of the Home tab and click on the arrow next to the Add or Remove Columns option. (This is the one in the center of the bottom row of that section that shows two sets of lines side by side with a dropdown arrow on the right-hand side.)

You can choose between One Column, Two Columns, Three Columns, or More Columns.

To split a list of values into two columns, select Two Columns. To change a list that is in multiple columns back to a single column, choose One Column.

When you click on More Columns you can specify not only the number of columns, but the spacing between them.

The way multiple columns work is that PowerPoint will fill the first column completely before it moves on to putting text into the second column. This means you may have to use extra enters to get half of your list into the second column. Otherwise you may end up with a column with ten entries next to a column with two entries. Better to go to the seventh line in that list and enter until six of your entries are in the first column and six are in the second column.

(If that sounded confusing, just try it in PowerPoint and it'll make more sense.)

Change Spacing Between Lines of Text

If you want to change the amount of space that appears between lines of text, you can do so by going to the Paragraph section of the Home tab and clicking on the arrow next to the Line Spacing option. This is the one with up and down arrows on the left-hand side of a group of lines that is located in the center of the top row.

Click on the arrow to see the available options, but be careful because it applies that space to any lines you have, even ones you might want to keep together.

Your other, and perhaps better, option is to right-click and choose Paragraph from the dropdown menu. This will bring up the Paragraph dialogue box. In the Spacing section you can specify the size of the space before and after each paragraph. This can be a way of putting space between bullet points or paragraphs while keeping the lines within a bullet point or paragraph close together.

Bullets and Numbering

By default, most of the templates include bullets within the main body of each presentation slide. If you want to change the type of bullet, turn off bullets for a specific line, add a bullet to a specific line, or change the bullets to numbers, then you can do so with the Bullets and Numbering options in the top left corner of the Paragraph section of the Home tab.

To change the type of bullet, click on the row you want to change or highlight all of your rows if there's more than one, and then go to the Bullets option (the one with dots next to lines in the top left corner of the Paragraph section of the Home tab) and click on the dropdown arrow.

You'll see a box around the type of bullet that's currently being used. Click on None if you don't want a bulleted list. Or click on one of the other options if you want to change the type of bullet. You can hold your cursor over each option to see what it will look like before you make your selection.

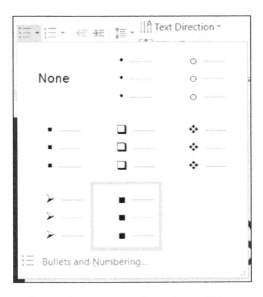

Clicking on Bullets and Numbering at the bottom of that list will let you specify the size of the bullet relative to the text as well as the color of the bullet. (But remember that the more you customize things, the more work you have to do throughout your presentation to keep everything uniform.)

If you want a numbered or lettered list instead (e.g., 1, 2, 3 or A, B, C) then click on the Numbering dropdown. There you can see a list of available numbered list options to choose from.

If you need to start at a number other than 1 or a letter other than A, click on Bullets and Numbering at the bottom of the list and then choose your starting point using the Start At box in the bottom right. For lettered lists (A, B, C) you enter a position number and it will change the letter. So a 1 equals A, a 2 equals B, etc. As with the bulleted list, you can also change the relative size of the number or letter compared to the list and change the color of the letter or number.

Another option for changing bullets or numbering is to right-click and go to either Bullets or Numbering in the dropdown menu.

Format Painter

If you ever find yourself in a situation where the formatting on one section of your presentation or your slide doesn't match another and you just want to take the formatting from one of the two and transfer it to the other, then the Format Painter is the easiest way to do so. It's located in the Clipboard section of the Home tab and looks like a little hand broom to me. (Given the name it's obviously a paintbrush.)

To use it, first highlight the text that's formatted the way you want. Next, click on the Format Painter. Then highlight the text that you want to be formatted that way. The formatting should transfer over, including font, font size, font color, line spacing, and type of bulleting/numbering.

Do not click anywhere else in between those steps and do not try to use the arrows to move between sections of text. Highlight, click, highlight. (Otherwise you might carry the formatting to the wrong text.)

This tool can be a lifesaver if someone has done weird things in a presentation you're trying to fix.

If the result isn't what you wanted or expected, then use Ctrl + Z to undo it and try again. Sometimes with paragraphs of text it can matter whether you selected the initial paragraph from the beginning or from the end. So if the formatting didn't transfer the way you thought it should, try selecting from the bottom of the paragraph up instead.

If you have more than one place you want to transfer formatting to, you can double-click on the Format Painter tool and then click on all of the text you want to change. It will stay selected until you click on it once more or hit Esc.

Other

As with formatting text you'll notice that there were a couple paragraph formatting options I didn't cover here. (SmartArt and Text Direction). If you do find yourself wanting to use either option they're available in the Paragraph section of the Home tab, but they shouldn't be needed for a basic presentation.

ADDING A TABLE TO A PRESENTATION SLIDE

Now that we've covered how to add text to your presentation and then format it, let's discuss how to add a table of data or a picture to your presentation.

If you look at a blank content slide that hasn't had any text added to it yet, you'll see in the center of the text box for most of these slides that there's a series of images. This is from a text box in a Two Content slide:

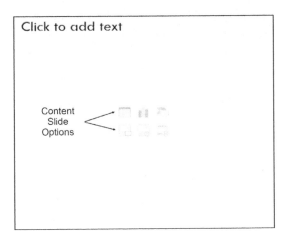

These are options you have other than just typing text into that box. Your options are Insert Table, Insert Chart, Insert a SmartArt Graphic, Pictures, Online Pictures, and Insert Video.

Once you choose one of these options you can't then type in that area. It's one or the other. (Although you could add a text box to the slide and put in text that way if you wanted. That's intermediate-level so we're not going to cover it here but the option can be found on the Insert tab in the Text section.)

We're not going to cover all of the non-text options in this guide, just adding a table and inserting a picture.

Let's start with the table option.

Insert Your Table

The first option in that set of images is to Insert Table.

Click on it and you'll see the Insert Table dialogue box. It lets you specify the number of columns and rows you want in your inserted table.

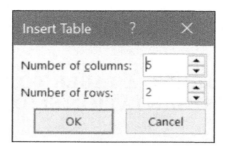

After you've chosen how many columns and rows you want, PowerPoint will insert a blank table with that number of columns and rows into that text box in your presentation. The first row will be formatted as a header row (so in a different color).

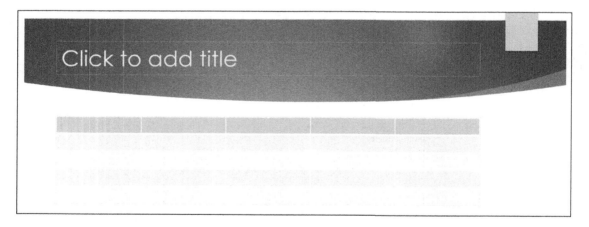

You can then click into any cell in that table to add your information. The colors used to create the table will match the theme you're using.

(If you look at each theme you'll see a set of colored squares at the bottom of the image for that theme. Those are the colors that are used for text, bullets, tables, and SmartArt for that theme. You can change that if you want under the Design tab under Table Tools, but the purpose of a theme is to use a coherent color scheme that all works together.)

Adding Text or Numbers to Your Table

To add text or numbers to your table, just go to the cell in the table where you want to add your text and start typing. If you enter text that is wider than the width of the column, it will automatically go to the next line and the row height will change to make sure all of the text is visible.

If you have the information in an existing table in Word or Excel, you can copy the information from that table into PowerPoint by highlighting the cells in Word or Excel, using copy (Ctrl + C), and then clicking into the first cell in the PowerPoint table where you want to place that information and using paste (Ctrl + V).

(This is sometimes the easier option when you have a lot of number formatting to do.)

Aligning Text Within Cells

If after you've entered text into your table you want to change the alignment of the text so that it's centered or left-aligned, etc. you can do this by highlighting the cells you want to change, going to the Layout tab under Table Tools, and going to the Alignment section. The top row where you see the three options with lines is where you can choose to left-align, center, or right-align text. The second row where you see the three boxes with lines in them is where you can choose to place text at the top, center, or bottom of each cell.

Adding Additional Rows or Columns

If you add a table and then want additional rows added to the table, simply use the tab key from the last cell in the last row of the table and PowerPoint will add a new line.

You can also highlight a row, go to the Layout tab under Table Tools, and choose Insert Above or Insert Below from the Rows & Columns section to add a row.

To add a column, highlight an existing column, go to the Layout tab under Table Tools, and choose Insert Left or Insert Right from the Rows & Columns section.

You can also highlight a row or column and right-click to bring up the mini formatting bar which has an Insert option with a dropdown arrow for inserting rows and columns.

Deleting a Row or Column

To delete a row or column from a table that you've decided you don't want, you can highlight the row or column, right-click and choose Cut or use the Delete option on the mini formatting bar.

Or you can click into a cell in that row or column, go to the Layout section of Table Tools, and under the Rows & Columns section click on the dropdown arrow under Delete. From there you can choose Delete Columns, Delete Rows, or Delete Table.

Deleting the Table

To delete the entire table, right-click and use the Delete option in the mini formatting bar to choose Delete Table. Or right-click on the table and choose Select Table from the dropdown and then use the Delete or Backspace key.

Or hold your mouse over the edge of the table until it looks like a four-sided arrow. Click on the table to select it and then use the Delete key or the Backspace key to delete it.

Moving the Table

Click on the table to select it or right-click and choose Select Table. Hold your mouse over the edge of the table until it looks like a four-sided arrow and then left-click and drag the table to where you want it.

Changing Column Width

To change the width of a column, click on a cell in the column and go to the Layout section of Table Tools and change the value in the Cell Size section for the Width.

You can also hold your mouse over the right-hand side of the column in the table itself until the cursor looks like two parallel lines with arrows pointing off to the sides and then left-click and drag to your desired width or double-left click to get the column to automatically resize to the width of the text that's currently in that column.

When you change the column width under Table Tools it will change just that column's width, so will also change the size of the table. Same with double-clicking to change the column width. If you use the click and drag option, both that column and the one next to it will have their column width changed but the overall size of the table will stay the same. That also means you can only click and drag so far because you'll be limited by the width of the two columns.

Changing Row Height

To change the height of a row, click on a cell in the row and go to the Layout section of Table Tools and change the value in the Cell Size section for the Height.

You can also hold your mouse over the bottom edge of the row in the table itself until the cursor looks like two parallel lines with arrows pointing up and down and then left-click and drag to your desired height. You will be limited in how skinny you can make a row based upon the font size for the text in the table.

With both methods, just that row's height will change so the table height will change as well.

Resizing the Table

To change the dimensions of an entire table, you can click on the table and then left-click and drag from any of the white squares around the edge of the table. Be sure that you have a white double-sided arrow when you do so or you may just ended up moving the table around. Clicking on one of the white boxes in the corner will allow you to resize the table proportionately as long as you click and drag at an angle.

You can also click on the table and go to the Layout tab under Table Tools and change the dimensions for the table listed under the Table Size section. If you want to resize the table and have the relative height and width of the table stay the same, click the Lock Aspect Ratio box first. When you do that PowerPoint will adjust both measurements at once to keep the ratio of height to width for the table constant.

Splitting Cells in a Table

You can take one or more cells in a table and split them into multiple cells. To do this, highlight the cell or cells you want to split, go to the Layout tab under Table Tools, and click on Split Cells in the Merge section. This will bring up the Split Cells dialogue box which lets you specify how many columns and rows you want each cell split into. This applies to each cell you selected. So if you select four cells and tell it to split them into two columns and one row, each of those four cells will be split into two columns and one row, so you'll have eight cells where there were four before.

You can also bring up the Split Cells dialogue box by highlighting the cells you want to split, right-clicking, and choosing Split Cells from the dropdown menu.

Merging Cells in a Table

You can also merge cells in a table. In this case, highlight the cells that you want to merge into one cell, go to the Layout tab under Table Tools, go to the Merge section, and choose Merge Cells.

You could also select the cells you want to merge, right-click, and choose Merge Cells from the dropdown menu.

ADDING A PICTURE TO A
PRESENTATION SLIDE

The option directly below Insert Table is Pictures. Click on it and you'll see the Insert Picture dialogue box. By default it will open in your Pictures folder on your computer, but you can navigate from there to any location on your computer where the picture you want is stored. If you click on the All Pictures dropdown option next to the File Name box you can see the picture file types that PowerPoint will accept. (Which looks to be pretty much any type you can image.)

Navigate to where the picture you want is saved, click on the picture, and then choose Insert.

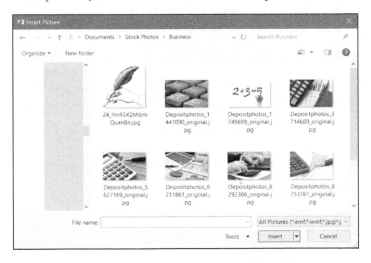

(There is an option there to link instead of insert your photo, but I'd advise against it because it's far too easy to break a link like that. Better to just put the image into your presentation.)

The image will insert into your slide at a size that fits within the text box where you chose to insert it. If the image is smaller than the active area it will insert at its current size, but if it's larger than the active area it will be scaled down and possibly cropped to fit.

(This is for when you use the Pictures icon to insert an image into a text box. You can also go to the Insert tab and choose Pictures from the Images section there to insert a picture on a blank slide.

In that case the image you insert will be centered in the presentation slide and may fit the entire slide if it's large enough.)

Moving a Picture

Once your image has been inserted into your slide, you can click on the image and drag it to the location you want. Left-click anywhere on the image, hold down the left-click, and drag the image to its new location. (It will take the text box it was inserted into with it, but if you then delete the image, the text box will reappear in its original location.)

Resizing a Picture

You can also resize a picture after you insert it into your slide. If you have specific dimensions that you want to use, click on the image and go to the Format tab under Picture Tools. On the far right-hand side you'll see the Size section.

Change either the height or the width and the image will resize proportionately. (So PowerPoint will adjust the other measurement to keep the height to width ratio the same.)

You can also click onto the image and then left-click on any of the white boxes around the perimeter and drag until the image is the size you want. This will not resize the image proportionately, so you can easily end up with a distorted image if you do it this way. But if you click on a corner and drag at an angle that usually will work because you are resizing the image on both the horizontal and vertical dimensions at once. (If you don't like the result, remember, Ctrl + Z to undo.)

Rotating a Picture

If you want to rotate the picture that you inserted, click on the image and then click on the little white outline of an arrow circling to the right that's above the image.

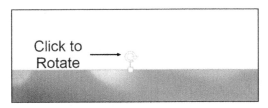

Click and hold this while you move your cursor in the direction you want to rotate the image and it will rotate along with your mouse.

Your other option is to click on the image and then go to the Format tab under Picture Tools and go to the Arrange section and choose Rotate. You can choose from the dropdown menu which lets you rotate 90 degrees right or left or flip the image vertically or horizontally. If you need more options than that, click on More Rotation Options to bring up the Format Picture task pane on the right-hand side of the screen. There you can set your rotation (the third option) to anything you want.

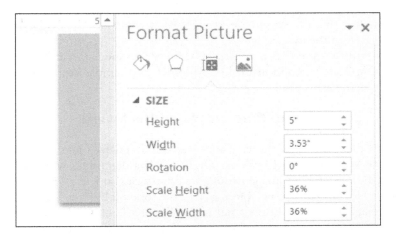

Cropping a Picture

Sometimes I'll drop a picture into a presentation and then realize that I didn't want the entire picture, I just wanted a section of it. (This is especially true when I take screenshots of Excel using Print Screen and then want to just keep a small section of that screenshot for my presentation.) In those cases, I need to crop the image to only show the portion I care about.

To crop an image, right-click on the image and choose Crop from the mini formatting bar. You should then see small black bars on each side of the image and at the corners. Left-click on those bars and drag until only the portion of the image that you want to keep is visible. Be sure when you click and drag that the cursor looks like a bar, because otherwise you might end up resizing the image instead. (If so, Ctrl + Z to undo and try again.)

When you move the boundaries of the image, you'll still see the full image but muted where it's no longer within your new boundaries.

You can click on the image and move it to make sure that the portion of the image you want to keep is within your new boundaries. (And if you insert an image that PowerPoint cropped and you want a different portion of that image to be visible, you can choose to "crop" the image and then click and drag until the portion of the image you wanted to be visible is, without actually changing the boundaries of the image.)

When you're satisfied that the cropped portion is what you want, hit Esc. You should now have just the cropped portion of the image.

Your other option for cropping is to go to the Format tab under Picture Tools and choose Crop from the Size section. The first option in the dropdown is a simple crop. You can also crop to a shape or crop to a specific aspect ratio.

Bring Forward/Send Backward

If you are ever in a situation where you have an image that overlaps a text box, you may need to use the bring forward or send backward options. These options determine which layer is visible when two layers overlap. If you have an image on top that you want in back, you send backward. If you have an image that's hidden that you need to move to the top you bring it forward.

Click on your image, go to the Format tab under Picture Tools, and go to the Arrange section. Choose either Bring Forward or Send Backward depending on what you need to do with the image. If there are multiple layers of images you can click on the arrow instead and choose to Bring to Front or Send to Back to make the image you've clicked the topmost layer or the backmost layer.

Alignment

Another option in the Arrange section of the Format tab is Align. There are a number of options available here. To align an image with respect to the presentation slide, click on the image and then click on the dropdown for Align.

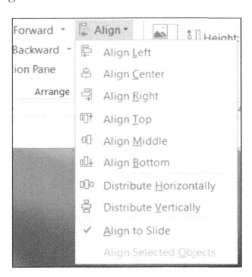

You can choose to align left (place the image along the left-hand side of the slide), align center (place the image in the center of the slide as judged from left to right), align right (place the image along the right-hand side of the slide), align top (place the image along the top edge of the slide), align middle (place the image in the center of the slide as judged from top to bottom), or align bottom (place the image along the bottom edge of the slide).

Distribute horizontally will center the image judged from left to right. Distribute vertically will center the image judged from top to bottom. Where this one matters is when you have multiple images selected at once. If you have multiple images selected at once then it will take those images and distribute them either across the width of the slide (horizontally) or from top to bottom (vertically) so that there is equal space between the images and the edges of the slide.

If you do have multiple images, you can select those images, and then under Align choose Align Selected Objects and instead of aligning the objects to the presentation slide it will align them to one another. So, for example, align right would move the left-hand object into alignment with the right-hand object.

Picture Styles

There is a Picture Styles section in the Format tab under Picture Tools. Click on your image to see what choices are available to you and then click on each style to see what it will look like in your slide. What these generally do is add borders or shading to your picture.

(I would recommend not using these unless you have a good reason to do so. I can't tell you how many times I've seen a presentation that had all sorts of added weirdness that distracted from what the presenter was trying to say. I'm a firm believer in keeping it simple.)

Adjusting a Picture

In the same way that I don't think you should use Picture Styles unless you need to, I'm going to advise against getting too fancy with adjusting a picture you import into your presentation, but I will point out the existence of the options for you. If you go to the Format tab under Picture Tools you'll see on the far left-hand side that there is a section called Adjust.

Click on the arrow under Corrections and you can see a series of options for sharpening or softening an image and for changing the brightness or contrast of the image. You can see what each option will look like as well.

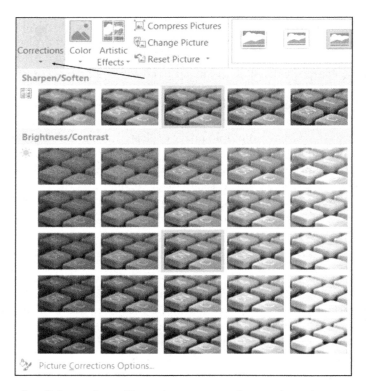

Click on the arrow under Color and you'll see that you can change the color saturation, color tone, or recolor your image.

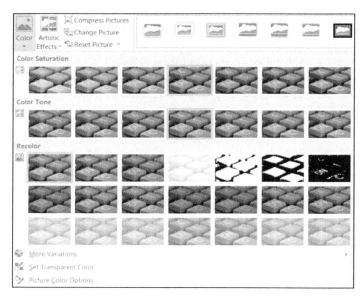

Click on the arrow under Artistic Effects and you'll see that you can apply a number of effects to your image.

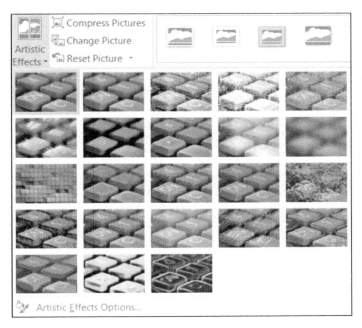

Once more, I wouldn't recommend doing this unless you have a good reason for doing so. Always ask yourself two questions before making a change like this. One, will it still look professional? (And professional means different things in different environments, so what's fine for an advertising agency will not be fine for an investment bank.) And, two, does what I just did make it easier for others to understand my presentation?

If it doesn't look professional, don't do it. And if it doesn't increase other people's ability to understand you, don't do it. The last thing you want is people more focused on what on earth that is than on what you're saying.

ANIMATIONS

If you have a presentation slide with multiple bullet points it's often very useful to have those bullet points appear one at a time. This way people listen to what you're saying instead of trying to read ahead on the slide and see what you're going to say.

The way you get one bullet point to appear on a slide at a time is by using the options under the Animations tab.

First, go to the slide where you want to add animation. Next, click on one of the lines of text and go to the Animations tab. From there click on one of the options in the Animation section.

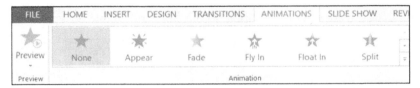

I recommend using Appear. It simply shows the line without any fancy tricks which can be distracting.

If the slide you're dealing with is just a list of bullet points with no indents and no images, the lines in the slide should now be numbered starting at one and up to however many lines you have.

This is the order in which they're going to appear as you give your presentation. (Usually triggered by hitting Enter, using the down arrow on your keyboard, or left-clicking to advance through the slide as you present.)

Item One

1 ▶ One item to compare

2 ▶ And more to say

3 ▶ And even more

4 ▶ And more than that

If you have indented lines of text you will probably need to fix their numbering. By default in my version of PowerPoint any indented lines share the numbering of their "parent" line. This is probably best understood visually. See below:

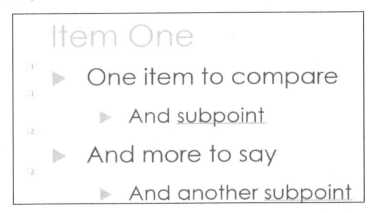

See how we have lines of text with indented lines below them? And how they are all numbered the same? So the first main line of text is 1 and so is its subpoint? And then the next is 2 and so is its subpoint?

That means the main line of text and the subpoint will appear in the presentation at the same time. But usually what I want is to make my main point and then make a subpoint.

To fix this, click into the slide, go to the Animations tab and click on the small arrow in the corner of the Animation section. This will bring up the Appear dialogue box.

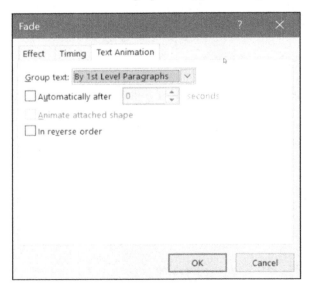

Go to the Text Animation tab and change the Group Text option. Depending on how many levels of bullets you have on the slide you will probably need the "By 2nd Level Paragraphs" or the "By 3rd Level Paragraphs" option to get all lines of text to appear individually. Click on OK.

The slide should now show adjusted numbering based upon your choice.

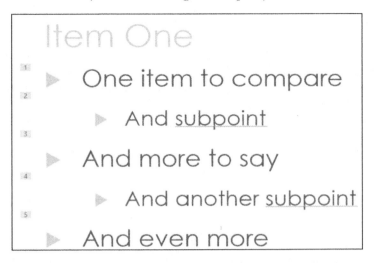

If you also have pictures in your slide, you need to be sure that the pictures are also going to appear or that it's okay that the picture appears first with no text. Also be careful to make sure that the picture appears in the order you want it.

If I have already numbered the lines of text in my slide and I click on a picture and then choose Appear from the Animation section of the Animations tab, it will be numbered last.

The easiest way to change the order in which your different elements appear on the slide is by going to the Animations tab and clicking on Animation Pane. This will bring up a pane on the right-hand side of the presentation slide that says Animation Pane.

It will show all of your elements and the order in which they appear. (You may have to click on the small double arrow under a numbered section to see all of your numbered options from your slide. In the image below I've already done that so clicking on it again would hide them.)

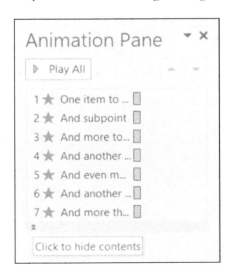

To change the order, click on one of the elements listed and then use the up and down arrows above the list of elements to move that element up or down.

You can also change the level at which your text is grouped in this pane by clicking on the arrow next to one of the text elements and then choosing Effect Options from the dropdown menu to bring up the Appear dialogue box. (Just remember that these choices are applied at the slide level, so any change you make in this manner will apply to all text elements on the slide.)

If you want to have some of your bullet points appear together but others appear separately, the best way I know to do this is to set up the slide as if everything will appear separately and then highlight the rows you want to appear together and click on your option in the Animation section of the Animations tab.

There are other things you can do with animation that we're not going to cover here, such as have each bullet point appear on its own on a timed schedule. But for this beginner guide I just wanted you to know how to structure your slides so that each point you want to make appears separately.

It's tempting to try to make a presentation more interesting with things like this, but if you can't engage your audience with what you're saying then fix what you're saying instead.

I would strongly urge you to keep to just using Appear as your animation option. You can have your bullet points fly in or even bounce in (please, no), but ask yourself if that's appropriate for your audience. If you're presenting to first graders, sure, have a bullet point bounce in. But a potential business client? Eh. Or a group of your professional peers? Uh-uh. Don't do it.

In a minute we'll talk about how to walk through your slides and see your animations in action, but first let's talk about a few general design principles I think are good to keep in mind.

BASIC DESIGN PRINCIPLES

I've touched on this a few times, but I think it's good to take a chapter and discuss some basic design principles to keep in mind as you're preparing your presentation. I'm going to assume here that you're actually intending to use your PowerPoint presentation as a presentation. Meaning, you're going to talk through it and not expect it to talk for you, and that the slides are going to be presented on a projector of some sort to a live audience.

(In other words, I'm not addressing the consulting model of using PowerPoint where you put together a weekly client presentation on a series of slides that you hand out to your client and pack full of information and then walk through even though the client could just read the darned things themselves without paying you thousands of dollars to be there while they do it.)

Font Size

Make sure that all of the text on your slide will be visible to anyone in the room. I'd try to have all of the text be 12 point or larger if you can manage it and with a strong preference for probably 16 point or above.

Font Type

As with all other design elements it can be tempting to use a fancy font. Resist the temptation. You want a basic, clear, easy-to-read font for your presentation elements. This means using something like Arial or Calibri or Times New Roman instead of something like Algerian or Comic Sans.

Summaries Instead of Explanations

The text on your slide should be there as a general outline of what you're going to say, not contain the full text of what you want to say. Think of each bullet point as a prompt that you can look at to trigger your recollection.

The reason you do it this way is because people will try to read whatever you put in front of them. So if you give them a slide full of text they will be busy reading that text rather than listening to what you have to say.

Also, if it's all on the slide, why listen to you at all?

So use the text on your slide as a high-level summary of your next point instead of as an explanation.

For example, I might have a slide titled "The Three Stages of Money Laundering" and then list on that slide three bullet points, "Placement", "Layering", and "Integration". As I show each bullet point I'll discuss what each of those stages is and how it works. If I feel a need to really go into detail then I'll have a separate slide for each one where I provide further information in small bite-sized chunks.

Contrast

You want your text to be visible. Which means you have to think about contrast. If you have a dark background, then use a light-colored text. For example, dark blue background, white text. If you have a light background, use a dark-colored text. For example, white background, black text.

And beware anything that could trip up someone with color-blindness. So no red on green or green on red and no blue on yellow or yellow on blue.

Also, and this may be more of a personal preference, but I try to use the slide templates that have white for the background behind the text portions of my slides. I'm fine with colorful borders and colorful header sections, but where the meat of the presentation is I prefer to have a white background often with black text. (That's the easiest combination to read.)

So I'll choose the Ion Boardroom theme before I'll choose the Ion theme, for example. That one's a perfect example.

Don't Get Cute

PowerPoint has a lot of bells and whistles. You can have lines of text that fly in and slide in and fade away. Or slides that flash in or appear through bars. And some of the templates it provides are downright garish.

Resist the urge to overdo it.

Ask yourself every time you're tempted to add some special effect if adding it will improve the effectiveness of your presentation. And ask yourself what your boss's boss's boss would think of your presentation. I've worked in banking and regulatory environments and I will tell you there is little appreciation in those environments for overly-bright colors and flashy special effects. (Whereas some tech company environment where the CEO wears jeans and t-shirts to work may be all for that kind of thing. Know your audience.)

I do think that using the animation option to have one bullet point appear at a time is a good idea. But you can do that with the Appear option. You don't need Fade, Fly In, Float In, Split, Wipe, etc.

And, yes, it can sometimes feel boring to use the same animation for a hundred slides in a row. But remember the point of your presentation is to convey information to your audience. Anything that doesn't help you do that should go.

ADDING NOTES TO A SLIDE

Now that we've walked through the basics of creating your presentation, let's cover a few other things you might want to do, starting with adding notes to your slides. You can print a notes version of the slides that lets you see each slide as well as your notes. This is a great approach when you have something very specific you want to say but that you don't want to put in the text of the slide.

So how do you add them?

In my version of PowerPoint the Notes portion of the presentation is not visible by default. But at the bottom of the slide I'm viewing there is the word Notes along the bottom border. If I click on this it reduces the size of the main slide and shows me a gray box that says "Click to add notes." If I click into that space and start typing those notes will go on the notes section for that slide.

The other option is to go to the Show section of the View tab and click on Notes. This will also reduce the size of the presentation slide and show the "Click to add notes" section.

Once the Notes section is visible you can click on the same option again to hide it.

OTHER TIPS AND TRICKS

Now that you understand the basics of putting together a PowerPoint presentation, let's discuss a few things you can do in PowerPoint that weren't covered elsewhere but that I think are worth knowing about as a beginning user.

Spellcheck

It's always a good idea to run spellcheck on anything you create for an audience. To check the spelling in your document, go to the Proofing section of the Review tab and click on Spelling. (It's on the far left-hand side.)

PowerPoint will then walk through your entire document flagging spelling errors and repeated words. For each one it will show you its suggested changes on the right-hand side of the screen and will highlight in the presentation slides the word that was flagged as having an error.

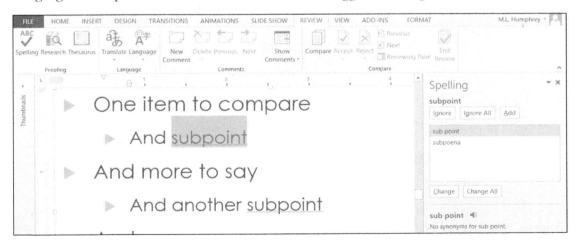

If you don't want to make the suggested change, click on Ignore. If PowerPoint has flagged a word, such as an unusual name, that is used multiple times throughout the document and you want it to ignore all uses of that word, you can choose Ignore All. (You can also choose Add to place it into your dictionary, but be careful with that because it will be added for all documents and that may not be what you want.)

For spelling errors PowerPoint will suggest possible words that you meant. Click on the word in the list that is the correct spelling and choose Change. If you're really bold you could do Change All and all misspellings of that word will be changed throughout the document, just be sure that's what you want.

Find

If you need to find a specific reference in your slides you can use Find to do so. The Find option can be found in the Editing section of the Home tab (on the far right-hand side). Click on Find and the Find dialogue box will appear.

You can also open the Find dialogue box by using Ctrl + F.

Type the word you want into the white text box and then click on Find Next. PowerPoint will walk you through the entire document moving to the next instance of that word each time you click on Find Next.

By clicking the boxes under the search term box, you can choose to just search for whole words only or to just search for words with the same capitalization (match case). This is useful with Find, but essential with Replace.

Replace Text

If you need to replace text within your slides you can use Replace. This essentially pairs the Find option with an option that takes the word you were searching for and replaces it with another. You can either launch the Replace dialogue box by using Ctrl + H or by going to the Editing section of the Home tab and clicking on Replace.

When you do this you'll see the Replace dialogue box. It has a text box for the text you want to find and a text box for what you want to replace that text with.

Once you've completed both boxes, click on Replace All to replace all instances of that word in your document. (Replace, when available, will replace only the next usage of the word.) If you don't complete the "replace with" box then you'll be deleting the text you chose to find.

With this one I strongly urge you to use match case and find whole words only. For example, let's say you wanted to replace the name Dan with Bob. Maybe Dan got fired and Bob took his place. (Bear with me, this is just to illustrate a point.) If you don't match case, then PowerPoint will replace every usage of dan with bob. That's probably not going to be a big issue, but if you don't look for whole words only then PowerPoint will take every dan in every word in your presentation and replace it with bob. So, for example, "danger" would become "bobger".

Replacing text is easy to do and easy to mess up. Be very, very careful if you choose to use it.

Replace Font

PowerPoint has a replace function that is unique to it and also incredibly useful. If you go to the Editing section of the Home tab and click on the dropdown arrow next to Replace you'll see that there is an option there to Replace Fonts.

Click on that option to bring up the Replace Font dialogue box.

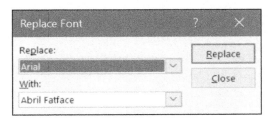

It will show you two dropdown menus.

The first menu is where you select the font that is in your presentation that you want to replace. It should only show the fonts used in your presentation. (Although it also kept showing me Arial whether it was used in the template or not and even after I'd replaced it with another font using the Replace font option.)

The second menu is where you choose the font you want to replace that font with. Once you do this and click on Replace, every usage of the first font will be replaced with the second font. This can come in very handy if you have a corporate requirement to use a specific font that wasn't followed when the presentation was created.

Just be sure to then look back through your presentation and make sure everything looks "right", because different fonts will take up different amounts of space on the page and it's possible that changing over the font could impact the appearance of your slides.

Presentation Size

PowerPoint gives you the choice between two presentation sizes. The standard size is 4:3 and the widescreen size is 16:9. You can also choose a custom slide size.

All of these choices are available in the Customize section of the Design tab on the far right side where it says Slide Size. Click on the dropdown arrow to make your choice.

(If you click on the Custom Slide Size option you can even make a presentation that is in portrait orientation, so like a normal printed report, rather than in landscape orientation. Although, if you're going to do this do it before you start putting together your slides or you'll have a complete mess to fix up. This would not be a good choice for a presentation that's going to be projected on a screen, but could be an interesting idea for a printed presentation.)

PRESENTING YOUR SLIDES

When it comes time to do your presentation, chances are someone will hook up a laptop with your presentation on it to a projector. By default that will show your computer screen. But you don't want someone to see what you've been seeing this whole time as you built your presentation. You just want them to see the slides and nothing else.

So when it comes time to present you need to go into presentation mode in PowerPoint.

To do this, go to the Slide Show tab.

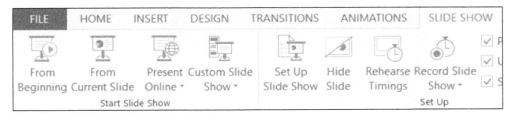

On the left-hand side you have the Start Slide Show section. If you click on From Beginning, this will start a presentation at the first slide in your PowerPoint presentation. If you click on From Current Slide it will start the presentation at the slide that's currently visible.

F5 will also start your presentation from the beginning. And Shift + F5 will start your presentation from your current slide.

Either choice will launch the slides you've created as a full-screen presentation.

The PowerPoint screen you've been working in will still be there and open behind the scenes. You can reach it using Alt + Tab to move through your active windows or you can use Esc to close the presentation version.

To navigate forward through the slides in your presentation, use the down arrow on the keyboard, Enter, or left-click. If you've added animations to your presentation then you'll move forward one animated section at a time. If not you'll move forward one slide at a time.

To move backward, use the up arrow on the keyboard. You can also right-click and choose Previous from the dropdown menu.

Before you enter presentation mode, I'd recommend having any additional windows you're going to want open already so you can easily access them using Alt + Tab.

And it's always a good idea to run through your presentation slides before you present to anyone so you can check and make sure that all the animations, etc. are working. You can do this on your computer screen easily enough by using F5 or the option to view the slideshow from the beginning.

Also—and I hesitate to mention this just because of the potential for things to go wrong and you to not be able to fix them in front of a crowd—there is an option to view your slides in Presenter View. What this is supposed to do is show on your computer screen the slide the audience can currently see as well as your slide notes and the next slide.

But there's a potential to accidentally display that information up on the screen for the audience instead. If that happens, at the top of the screen there is an option at the top of the presenter screen to choose Display Settings and then Swap Presenter View and Slide Show.

If you want to try using Presenter View, right-click on your slide when in presentation mode and choose Show Presenter View from the dropdown menu.

To close a presentation, hit Esc. Or right-click and choose End Show from the dropdown menu.

PRINTING YOUR PRESENTATION

To print your presentation, handouts, or slides with notes, you can type Ctrl + P or go to the File tab and then choose Print on the left-hand side. Both choices will bring you to the same location.

You have a number of print options on the left-hand side and then a preview of what the page will look like when you print it on the right-hand side.

The default is to print all of your slides and in full-page format and that's what your preview will show. But let's walk through everything you can see on this page and your other possible print options.

Print

Right at the top of the page under the Print header is the printer icon. It shows a printer and says Print under it. This is what you click when you're ready to print your document.

Copies

Next to that is where you specify the number of copies to print. By default the number to print is 1, but you can use the arrows on the right-hand side of the text box to increase that number. (Or decrease it if you've already increased it.) You can also just click into the white text box and type the number of copies you need.

Printer

Below those two options is the Printer section. This is where you specify the printer to use. It should be your default printer, but in some corporate environments you'll want to change your printer choice if, for example, you need the color printer.

To do this, click on the arrow on the right-hand side. This will bring up a dropdown menu with all of your printers listed. Click on the one you want. If the one you want isn't listed then use Add Printer to add it.

Printer Properties

If you want to print on both sides of the page you'll need to specify this using Printer Properties which is the blue text visible under the name of the printer. Clicking on that text will bring up a Document Properties dialogue box.

Click on the Layout tab and choose from the dropdown under Print on Both Sides to choose whether to print on both sides of the page and how. If the paper orientation is Portrait, choose Flip on Long Edge. If the paper orientation is Landscape, choose Flip on Short Edge.

You don't need to change the other properties here because they're available on the main screen.

Print All Slides/Print Selection/Print Current Slide/Custom Range

Your next option is what to print. By default, you'll print all the slides in the presentation.

If you were clicked onto a specific slide in the presentation and want to just print it then you can choose Print Current Slide. (When you choose this the print preview should change to show just that one slide.)

If you had selected more than one slide in the presentation and then chose to print, you can choose Print Selection to print those slides.

Your other option is print a custom range. The easiest way to use this one is to type the slide numbers you want into the Slides text box directly below the dropdown. This will automatically change the dropdown selection to Custom Range. Your preview will also change to just show the slides you've listed.

You can list numbers either individually or as ranges. If you list a range you use a dash between the first and last number. So 1-10 would print slides 1 through 10. You can also use commas to separate numbers or ranges. So 1, 2, 5-12 would print slides 1, 2 and 5 through 12.

Full Page Slides/Notes Pages/Outline/Handouts

The next choice is what you want to print.

In the top section you can choose to print full page slides, notes pages, or an outline.

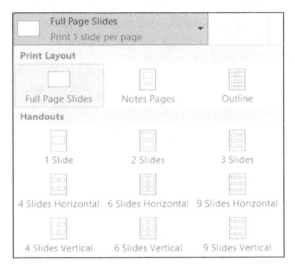

Full page slides will put one slide on each page you print and nothing else.

Notes pages will put one slide per page on the top half of the page and your notes on the bottom half of the page. Each page will be in portrait orientation. (Short edge on the top.)

Outline will take all of the text from your slides and list it out in the same way it's listed on the slides. So if there are bullet points, the outline will have them, too. If there aren't, it won't. Each printed page will contain multiple slides' worth of information. No images are included.

If you want to provide handout slides, you have a number of options to choose from. The one slide option will center each presentation slide in the middle of a page in portrait orientation. (Not recommended.) The two slide option will put two slides on each page in portrait orientation. (This is a good choice for handouts because it's still visible but doesn't waste paper the way the one-slide option does.)

You can put as many as nine slides on the page, but before you do that think about how legible that will be for the end-user. If you have a lot of slides with images it might be fine, but if they have a lot of text on them or if people will need/want to take a lot of notes, no one is going to thank you for putting nine slides on a page.

The horizontal and vertical choices determine whether the slides are ordered across and then down (horizontal) or down and then across (vertical). I think, at least in the U.S., that most people would expect horizontal.

Collated/Uncollated

This only matters if you're printing more than one copy of the presentation. In that case, you need to decide if you want to print one full copy at a time x number of times (collated) or if you want to print x copies of page 1 and then x copies of page 2 and then x copies of page 3 and so on until you've printed all pages of your document (uncollated).

In general, I would recommend collated, which is also the default.

Portrait Orientation/Landscape Orientation

This determines whether what you've chosen to print prints with the long edge of the page at the top or the short end of the page at the top. In general, PowerPoint chooses this for you and does a good job of it. For example, outline should be portrait and full page slides should be landscape.

However, you might want to change this for the handout slides. For one slide, four slide, and nine slide printing, I think landscape is a better choice than portrait. You can judge for yourself by looking at the preview and seeing how large the slides are and how much white space is taken up with each orientation.

Color/Grayscale/Pure Black and White

This option lets you choose whether to print your slides in color or not. The choice you make will probably depend on your available print resources. When you change the option you'll see in the print preview what each one looks like. The grayscale and pure black and white options seem to strip colored backgrounds out of the presentation. The pure black and white one strips color out of the header sections as well.

Edit Header & Footer

At the very bottom of the list you can click on the text Edit Header & Footer to bring up the Header and Footer dialogue box where you can choose to add the date and time, slide number, or a customized footer display to your printed document

Only the Notes and Handouts slides can have a header on them and that's specified on a separate tab.

Once you choose to apply your choices, you can see how it will look in the print preview.

WHERE TO LOOK
FOR OTHER ANSWERS

My goal in this guide was to give you a solid understanding of how PowerPoint works and the tools to create a basic presentation. But there are a number of topics I didn't cover in this guide, such as how to change a presentation slide background color, creating a custom design template, adding timing to your presentation slides, or adding objects or text boxes to a slide.

At some point you'll probably want to learn about one of these things.

So how do you do it? Where do you get these answers?

First, in PowerPoint itself you have a few options. You can hold your cursor over the choices in any of the tabs and you'll usually see a brief explanation of what that choice can do. For example, here is the New Slide option in the Home tab:

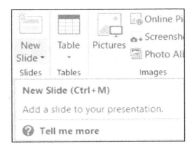

You can see that it says this option will let you "add a slide to your presentation." If that brief description isn't enough, a lot of the options have a Tell Me More option below that. Click on that text and the built-in Help function in PowerPoint will open giving a more detailed description of what you can do.

Another option is to go directly to the built-in Help function. You do this by clicking on the question mark in the top right corner of the screen or pressing F1. This will launch PowerPoint Help. From there you can either navigate to what you want or type in a search phrase in the search box.

I often find myself needing more information than this so turn to the internet. If I need to know the mechanics of how something works, the Microsoft website is the best option. For example, if I wanted to understand more about the colors used in each theme in PowerPoint I might search for "colors powerpoint theme microsoft 2013".

It's key that you add the powerpoint, microsoft, and your version year in your search.

When I get my search results, I then look for a search result that goes to support.office.com. There will usually be one in the top three or four search results.

If that doesn't work or I need to know something that isn't about how things work but can I do something, (and this is more true probably in Excel than in PowerPoint), then I will do an internet search to find a blog or user forum where someone else had the same question. Often there are good tutorials out there that you can read or watch to find your answer.

And, of course, you can also just reach out to me at mlhumphreywriter@gmail.com.

I don't check that email daily but I do check it regularly and I'm happy to track down an answer for you or point you in the right direction.

CONCLUSION

So there you have it. We've covered the basics of PowerPoint and at this point in time you should be able to create your own nicely polished basic presentation.

PowerPoint is great for presentations. And it's a valuable skill to have. I've used PowerPoint both in my corporate career as well as my writing career. If you're going to stand in front of a room of fifty (or five hundred) people it's nice to have a presentation up on a screen to help you stay focused on what you meant to say. (And it keeps you from staring down at a podium the whole time while you read your notes.)

It also gives your audience something to look at other than you.

Having said that, you'll have seen in this guide that I have some definite opinions about how PowerPoint presentations can be misused and abused. It can be fun to put a ton of crazy colors and shapes into your presentation and have things bouncing in and zooming out and flashing around, but resist that temptation.

Remember that PowerPoint is a tool, and that its purpose is to help you convey information to your audience. Anything you do in your presentation that takes away from your ability to convey information is a bad thing.

So exercise restraint. (Unless you're in a setting where a lack of restraint will help you, like a presentation to three hundred first graders…In that case, go wild.)

Anyway. Good luck with it. And reach out if you get stuck. I'm happy to help.

ABOUT THE AUTHOR

M.L. Humphrey is a former stockbroker with a degree in Economics from Stanford and an MBA from Wharton who has spent close to twenty years as a regulator and consultant in the financial services industry.

You can reach M.L. at mlhumphreywriter@gmail.com or at mlhumphrey.com.

Made in the USA
Monee, IL
04 December 2021